A NOTE TO MUSICIANS:

Besides the piano score,
most of the songs in this book
feature simple guitar chords.

TM & copyright © by Dr. Seuss Enterprises, L.P. and Eugene Poddany 1967.
Copyright renewed 1995 by Dr. Seuss Enterprises, L.P. and Oleg Poddany

All rights reserved.
Published in the United States by Random House Children's Books,
a division of Penguin Random House LLC, New York.

Random House and the colophon are registered trademarks of
Penguin Random House LLC.

Visit us on the Web!
Seussville.com
randomhousekids.com

Educators and librarians, for a variety of teaching tools, visit us at
RHTeachersLibrarians.com

ISBN 978-0-394-81695-1

Library of Congress Control Number: 67-21921

Printed in the United States of America
17 16 15 14 13 12 11 10 9

THE CAT IN THE HAT SONGBOOK

BY Dr. Seuss

Piano Score and Guitar Chords by Eugene Poddany

Random House ⌂ New York

For Lark and Lea
of
Ludington Lane

LET US ALL SING

Slowly and deliberately

Let us all sing! It's good for al - most an - y thing. It's

in a bright sprightly tempo

good for dus - ty mus - ty throats to let out gus - ty lus - ty notes. It's

good for peo - ple, frogs and goats to o - pen up and sing. It's

good for tongues and necks and knees of peo - ple, bees and chim - pan - zees. So,

The Super-Supper MARCH

3. Oys - ters, noo - dles, straw - ber-ry stroo - dles, French fries, fish hash, one red beet.

4. Do - nuts, dump-lings, blue - ber-ry bump- lings, choc' - late mush-mush, su - per sweet.

Lamb chops, wham chops, huck-le- ber- ry mish mash, Oh, the things that I could eat!

Clam stew, ham stew, wa-ter-mel- on wush wush,

Oh, the stuff that I could eat! Deep dish rhu - barb up - side - down cake,

MY UNCLE TERWILLIGER

Easy waltz tempo

ritard

My

a tempo

mf Un - cle Ter - wil - li - ger waltz - es with bears _____

WALTZES WITH BEARS

It's a ter - ri - ble, ter - ri - ble state of af -
Un - cle says it's more fun than just sit - ting in

fairs. _____ Ev - ery Sat - ur - day night, he creeps
chairs, _____ and I'm not going to stop it, my

Mysterioso

down our back stairs, sneaks out of our house to go
un - cle de - clares, It keeps my mind off of my

1. Emi.⁶ Edim. D A D

stop   him from wa - wa - wa,   waltz - ing   with   bears! _____

F C⁷ F C⁷

slightly boisterous

2. My

f

r. h.

2. Emi.⁶ Gmi.⁶ D A⁷ Adim. A⁷ Gmi.⁶ D

ritard

stop   him from wa - wa - wa,   waltz - ing   with   bears!

r. h.

In My Bureau Drawer

Not too fast

I once knew a fel-low who had twelve teeth, five up on top, and five un-der-neath, and one in his pock-et and that left one more that he kept back home in his

The No LAUGH

RACE

A Party Game Song

Note: This is an elimination contest. Any child who laughs has to drop out. The leftover children regroup with new partners. They keep this up until only one child, the winner, remains.

no - laugh race is a - bout to start. Stand face to face, three in - ches a - part.

if you need a fel-low who can plunk and plink, I'm the

plunk-plunk plunk-er that you need!

Plink, plink!

spoken
Plink - plink! Plunk - plunk! Plink - Plink, plink!

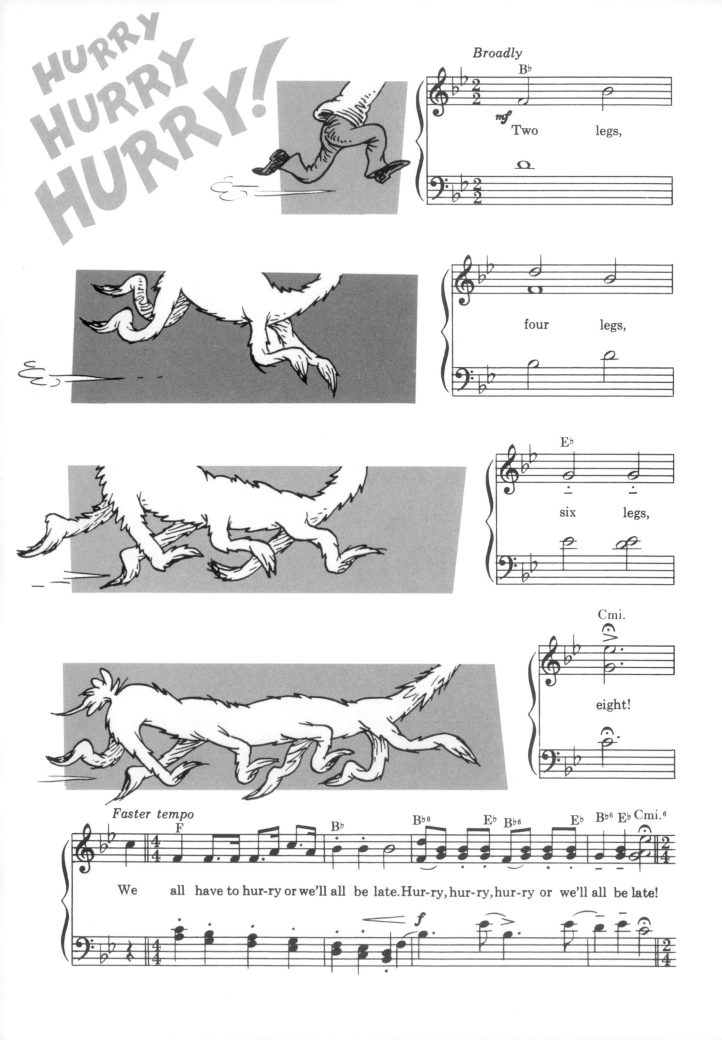

Two legs, four legs, six legs, eight!

slower

But when you hur-ry fast, you be-gin to puff and blow. And your legs won't last, so we'd

Gradually slower and slower

bet-ter hur-ry slow. So let's be late, that's what we'll do, with our

Finally dragging to a stop

eight legs, six legs, four legs, two!

CRY

Slowly with exaggerated pathos

Gmi. Cmi. Gmi. Cmi. D⁻⁹ D⁷

mp

I'm so

Gmi.

sad   I could cry a   pint _____ A

Ped.

Cmi.   Cmi.⁷ D⁷ Gmi.

pint of tears _____ I _ might, I   might. _____ Boo -

A PINT

hoo. Boo - hoo. Boo - hoo. Boo - hoo. A

pint of tears. _____ Boo - hoo. Boo - hoo. *(sigh)* Boo -

hoo! _____ *un poco più mosso* Now I'm

A·A·A·H...

*NOTE: strike keyboard with open palms of hands

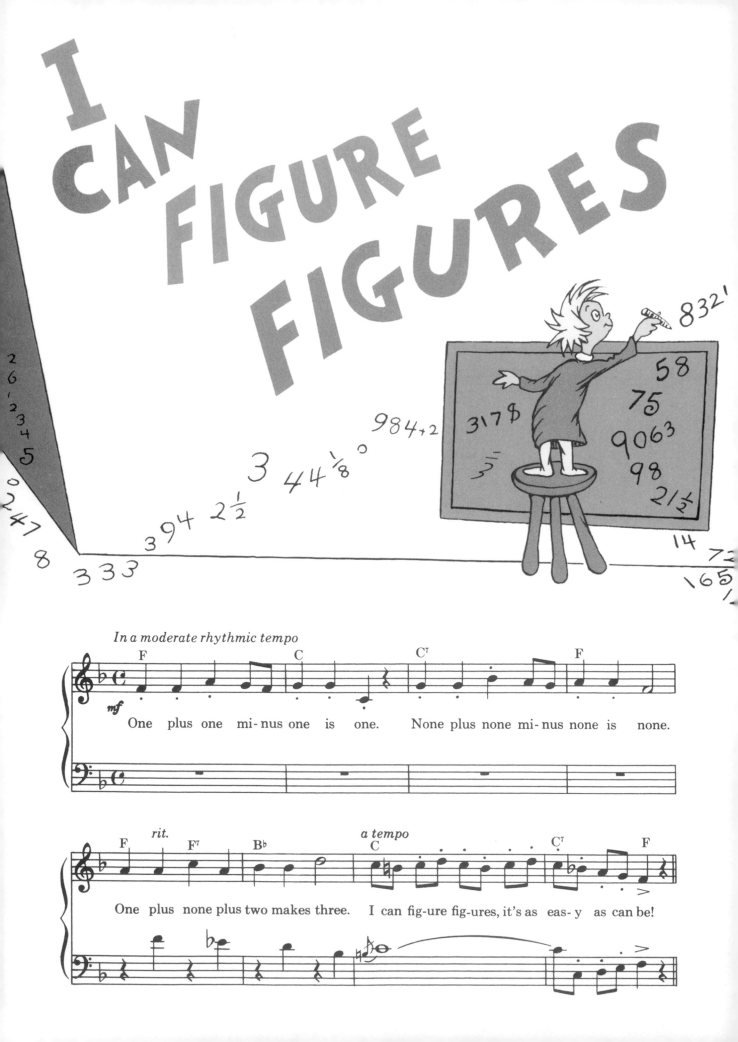

Andante doloroso

Some-bod-y stole my hoo-to foo-to boo-to bah,___ and I'm ver-y ver-y

sad. It was the on- ly hoo-to foo-to boo-to bah___

___ that I ev-er, ev-er had. I can't do a thing with-out my

with Pedal   *p dolente*

STOLE MY HOO-TO FOO-TO BOO-TO BAH!

hoo-to foo-to boo-to bah _____ can't eat, can't sleep _____ with-out my

hoo-to foo-to boo-to bah. I can't wash or go to school. I'll end

up as a fool! Oh please, bring my hoo-to foo-to boo-to bah back. _____

a bit faster and louder · · · · · · · · · · *simile staccato*

mp
Dib-ble, dib-ble, dib-ble, drip, drip, drip. Dob-ble, dob-ble, dob-ble, drop, drop, drop!

Drip. Dib-ble, dib-ble. Drop. Dib-ble, dib-ble, dib-ble, dib-ble, dib-ble, drip, drip, drip!

* Drop. Dob-ble, dob-ble. Drop. Dob-ble, dob-ble, dob-ble, dob-ble, dob-ble, drop, drop, drop!

mf   *ritard*
Dib-ble, dib-ble, dib-ble, dib-ble, dib-ble, dib-ble, dob-ble, dob-ble, dob-ble, dob-ble, drop, drop!

develop into a mighty storm
Dib-ble, drip, drip! Dib-ble, drip, drip! Dib-ble, dib-ble, dib-ble, drip, drip, drip!

f *with pedal*

**NOTE: *voices should sing top notes of right hand
an octave lower, wherever this extreme register is encountered.*

tempo as in beginning

mp

Drip,   drip, drip,   drip,   drip, drip. Dib - ble, dib - ble, dib - ble, drip, drip, drip!

Drop, drop, drop,   drop,   drop, drop.   Dob - ble, dob - ble,   drop, drop!

(gradually slower and diminuendo)

p

Drop, drop.   Drip.   Drop.   *pp*   *l.h.*

Plop!

To Little SALLY SPINGEL SPUNGEL SPORN

SALLY

With expression

mp

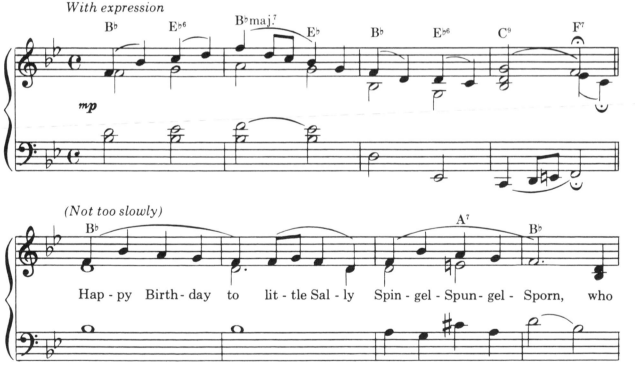

(Not too slowly)

Hap - py Birth - day to lit - tle Sal - ly Spin - gel - Spun - gel - Sporn, who

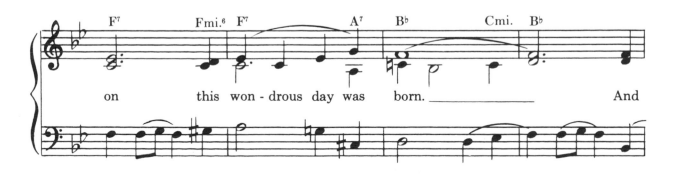

on this won - drous day was born. _____ And

with your left sock down. They reach a - round dark

cor - ners, when you stroll a - bout at night. Then,

woosh! There goes your left sock. And you're left there with your

right! _____ And when the left sock thiev- ers _

make a left sock theft,

feel - ing kind of fool - ish

you'll be

with your right sock left!

DRUMMING

A ROUND

In a crisp marching tempo
(FIRST VOICE)

Rap! Tap, tap, tap. Rap! Tap, tap, tap.

Rat - tle tat - tle. Rat - tle tat - tle. Need a lit - tle rat - tle tat - tle.

Boom, boom! Boom, boom! Need a lit - tle boom, boom. Rat-tle tat - tle. Tap. Tap.

voices tacet last time

Boom, boom, boom! Rap! Tap, tap, tap. Rap! Tap, tap, tap.

in this measure eliminate voices one at a time in reverse order of entry, (1st voice finishes last)

(piano finishes alone)

PARTY

PARTING

Slow and Sentimental

Time goes past. Time goes fast. Comes a time in ev-'ry par-ty

when the par-ty parts. Good time ends. Good night, good friends. Good

night to all your warm and friend-ly fool - ish hearts. So

Brighter and faster

rum-ble, rum-ble, rum-ble home now. Rum-ble, rum-ble, rum-ble